A 3-minute forever book

EAT
YOUR
PEAS®

for Grandparents

By Cheryl Karpen
Gently Spoken Communications

Being pretty on the inside means
you don't hit your brother
and you
eat all of your peas
⌒ that's what
my grandma taught me.

-Lord Chesterfield

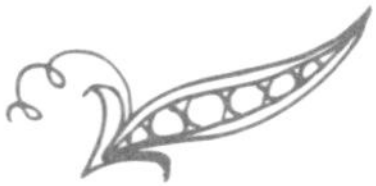

A special gift for

_____

from

_____

At the heart
of this little book
is a promise.

It's a promise from
me
to
you
and it goes like this:

No matter the
miles or distance between us,
I promise
I will always hold our memories,
the lessons you taught me
and
your love
close to my heart.

Meanwhile,
may this little book
help me express
my love and admiration.

Nana, Papa, Grandma, Grandpa...

you will always be

grand

to me.

I love you.

I love you.

I love you.

The first time
I saw you,
I knew
you loved me, too.

Like the loving stitches
of a quilt
you connect us
to what really matters.

Each other. Our stories.
The heart of who we are.

Going to your house is like
going away and coming home
at the same time.

Your house is
Holidays * Hideaways * Adventures * Hugs

You have a way of sending sunshine into my heart.

I admire you for your

strength

wisdom

courage

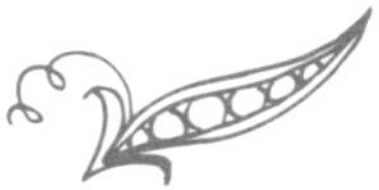

There's nobody else like you.

Anywhere. Anyplace.

Opening a card or letter
(e-mail, too)
from you

always makes my heart
beat a little faster.

Thank you
for making me feel
special and important.

May I do the same for you!

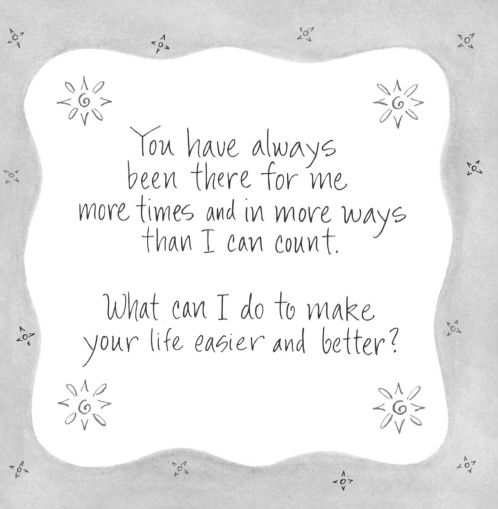

You have always
been there for me
more times and in more ways
than I can count.

What can I do to make
your life easier and better?

Keep this little book
where you can see it often.

Let it be a reminder
Someone (me)
is thinking
fondly of you.

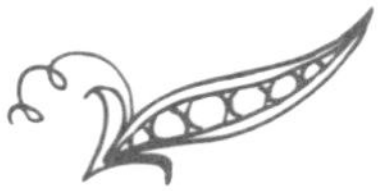

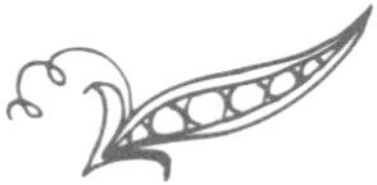

Now it's my turn to
believe in
you
and those
dreams
that still need doing.

It's time to do what you love
(for the first time or all over again!)

To be good to yourself
(and let others be good to you, too.)

To nap in the sun
(or take a walk in the country.)

Oh, and one more thing...

Remember to always...

Eat Your Peas!

Why Peas?

She was a vibrant, dazzling young woman with a promising future.
Yet, at sixteen, her world felt sad and hopeless.

I was living over 1800 miles away and wanted to let this very special young person in my life know I would be there for her across the miles and through the darkness. I wanted her to know she could call me any time, at any hour, and I would be there for her. And I wanted to give her a piece of my heart she could take with her anywhere—a reminder she was loved.
Really loved.

Her name is Maddy and she was the inspiration for my first PEAS book, **Eat Your Peas for Young Adults.** At the very beginning of her book I made a place to write in my phone number so she knew I was serious about being available. And right beside the phone number I put my promise to listen—really listen—whenever that call came.

Soon after the book was published, people began to ask me if I had the same promise and affirmation for adults. I realized it isn't just young people who need to be reminded how truly special they are. We all do.

Today Maddy is thriving and giving hope to others in her life.
If someone has given you this book, it means you are pretty special to them and they wanted to let you know. Take it to heart.

Believe it, and remind yourself often.

Wishing you peas and plenty of joy,

Cheryl Karpen

P.S. If you are wondering why I named the collection, Eat Your Peas…it's my way of saying, "Stay healthy. I love and cherish you. I want you to live **forever!**"

A portion of the profits from the
Eat Your Peas Collection
will benefit empowerment programs
for youth and adults.

With gratitude...

To illustrator and dear friend,
Sandy Fougner
for gracing each page
with her loving artistry.

To amazing editor,
Suzanne Foust
for always knowing the
right thing to say.

A special thank you
to the "grand" ladies
of The Palms of Islamorada:
Dora, Joy, Gerry, and Nancy
for their insight and wisdom.

~Cheryl

About the author

"Eat Your Peas"

A self-proclaimed dreamer, Cheryl
spends her time imagining and creating
between the historic river town of Anoka, Minnesota
and the seaside village of Islamorada, Florida.

An effervescent speaker, Cheryl brings inspiration,
insight, and humor to corporations,
professional organizations and churches.
Learn more about her at: www.cherylkarpen.com

About the illustrator

Sandy Fougner artfully weaves
a love for design, illustration and
interiors with being a wife
and mother of three sons.

The Eat Your Peas Collection™

Takes only 3-minutes to read but you'll want to hold on to it forever!

Eat Your Peas for Grandkids
Eat Your Peas for Daughters
Eat Your Peas for Sons
Eat Your Peas for Someone Special
Eat Your Peas for Tough Times
Eat Your Peas for Birthdays
Eat Your Peas for Teens
Eat Your Peas for Girlfriends
Eat Your Peas for New Moms
Eat Your Peas for Sisters
Eat Your Peas for Me
Eat Your Peas for Mothers
Eat Your Peas for Fathers
Eat Your Peas for Sweethearts
Eat Your Peas for the Holidays

New titles are SPROUTING up all the time!

To view a complete collection, visit us on-line at www.eatyourpeas.com

Eat Your Peas® for Grandparents

Copyright 2006, Cheryl Karpen

Printed in the USA

For more information or to locate a store near you, contact:
Gently Spoken
PO Box 245
Anoka, MN 55303

Toll-free 1-877-224-7886 or visit us on-line at
www.eatyourpeas.com